The Enchanted Mandala
Coloring Book

The Enchanted Mandala Coloring Book

SIRIUS

SIRIUS

This edition published in 2024 by Sirius Publishing, a division of
Arcturus Publishing Limited,
26/27 Bickels Yard, 151–153 Bermondsey Street,
London SE1 3HA

ISBN: 978-1-3988-4488-9
CH011994NT
Supplier 29, Date 0524, PI 00006498

Printed in China

Introduction

The repeating circular patterns of mandalas make them one of the most soothing subjects for coloring. They are found in many religions, including Hinduism, Buddhism, Shinto, and Jainism. They may be a map to show spiritual places, as well as gods in some religions, and sometimes the location of shrines. Buddhism sometimes uses a mandala to show the whole universe, with the sacred Mount Meru, with its five peaks, at its heart. Carl Jung used mandalas as part of his practice, considering it as a representation of the self.

The spiritual journey represented by a mandala starts at its outer edge, moving through the layers to reach the inner core. You can color each layer in the same palette for a soothing way to reflect as you color.

The designs here range from the pure and simple to the exquisitely complex. All you need are your pens or pencils, and your powers of concentration.

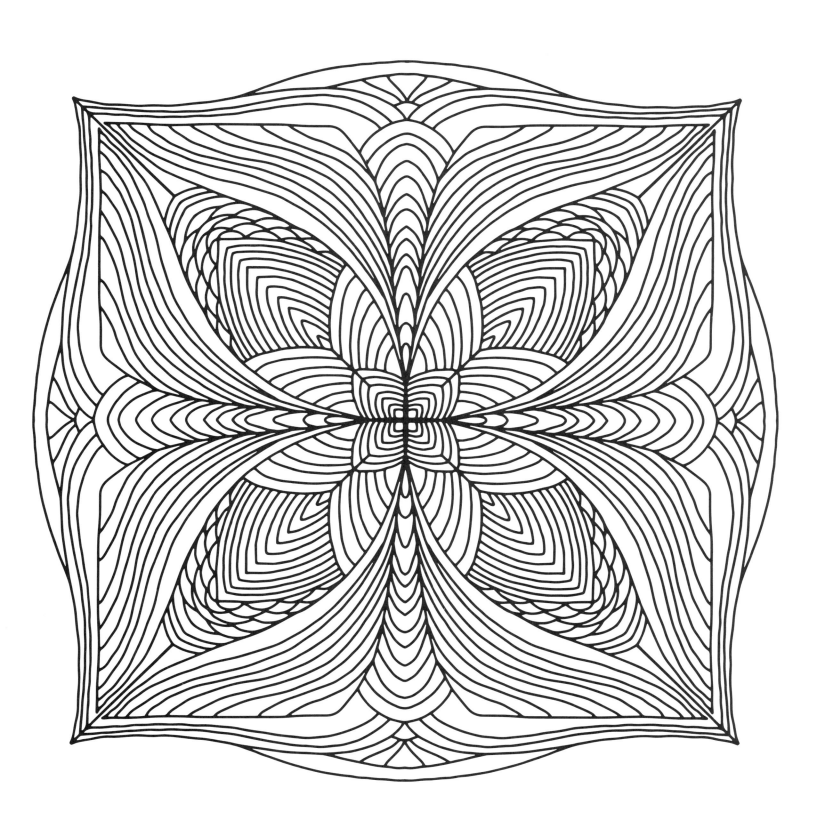